THE HOW TO FOR

THE DO IT YOURSELFER

RETRO FIT

WINDOWS

THE HOW TO FOR

THE DO IT YOURSELFER

RETRO FIT

WINDOWS

Z-BAR (FLUSH FIN) APPLICATIONS

FOR THE REPLACEMENT OF OLD ALUMINUM AND STEEL WINDOWS

JOSE A. BARRAGAN

Library of Congress Control Number: 2012905767
ISBN: Hardcover   978-1-4691-8796-9
                 Softcover   978-1-4691-8795-2
                 Ebook   978-1-4691-8797-6

To order additional copies of this book, contact:
Xlibris Corporation
1-888-795-4274
www.Xlibris.com
Orders@Xlibris.com
113413

CONTENTS

STEPS FOR RETRO FIT WINDOW INSTALLATION, Z-BAR (FLUSH FIN)

NOTES

Step 1: What kind of window do you have?

(XO   OX   XOX)

O is the stationary window and X is the sliding window. View window from the outside to determine X and O.

Example:

View from outside

Opening Side	fixed panel (does not Open)
X	**O**

fixed panel (does not Open)	Opening Side
O	**X**

NOTES

Step 2: Measuring for your New Retro Fit Window (Width x Height)

Key notes:

(Your New Retro Fit Window will fit inside your old window frame)
(Never remove the old frame)
(When measuring you must always measure the width first and then the height)

The old window frame consists of Three Parts.

The Inner   — (holds X in place and keeps the sliding window from falling into the home).

The Middle — (Separates X and O)

The outer   — (Holds O in place and keeps the window from falling outside the home).

NOTES

To determine the Width of your new window, you must measure frame to frame.

The Inner, The Middle, and The Outer parts.

Once you have done so, choose the smallest measurement and subtract ½" inch because you need a ¼" inch space on either side of the window for proper adjustment.

Example:

56" Width 56"—½" = 55 ½"
Width of new window is 55 ½"

NOTES

To determine the Height of your new window, you must measure frame to frame.

The Inner, The Middle, and The Outer parts.

Once you have done so, choose the smallest measurement and subtract ½" inch because you need a ¼" inch space on either side of the window for proper adjustment.

Example:

34" Height 34"—½" = 33 ½"
Height of new window is 33 ½"

Example:

Window size 55 ½" x 33 ½"
(This is the size that the new window will be ordered at)

NOTES

Step 3: Make sure the Z-Bar (Flush Fin) will cover the old window frame.

If the Z-Bar (Flush Fin) does not cover the old window frame you will need to order your window with a wider Z-Bar (flush Fin).

You may even have to change the window company if they do not carry the size you need.

NOTES

I. Add 3" to your measurement because the smallest Z-Bar (flush Fin) is 1 ½" wide on either side.

Example:

[55 ½" + 3"] x [33 ½" + 3"] = 58 ½" x 36 ½"

NOTES

II. Go outside to measure the old window frame from the outer edge to outer edge (Width x Height).

If the measurement is less than your window size plus 3", you Do Not have to order a wider Z-Bar (flush Fin).

If the measurement is greater than your window size plus 3", you Do have to order a wider Z-Bar (flush Fin).

If you do in fact have to order a wider Z-Bar (flush Fin), you must measure your Z-

Bar (flush Fin) and double its measurement.

Once you have done so, you must add that measurement to your window size.

Example:

Z-Bar (flush Fin) sizes 1 ½", 1 ¾", 2", 2 ¼" . . . Etc

$$1 \frac{1}{2}" + 1 \frac{1}{2}" = 3"$$
Then add 3" to your window size.

NOTES

$$1 \tfrac{3}{4}" + 1 \tfrac{3}{4}" = 3 \tfrac{1}{2}"$$
Then add 3 ½" to your window size.

$$2 + 2 = 4"$$
Then add 4" to your window size.

$$2 \tfrac{1}{4}" + 2 \tfrac{1}{4}" = 4 \tfrac{1}{2}"$$
Then add 4 ½" to your window size.

You must repeat the process until you find the size that will work for you.

Key Note:

It is always better to have a wider Z-Bar (flush Fin) than needed.

NOTES

Step 4: Order your Retro Fit Z-Bar (flush Fin) window(s).

NOTES

Step 5: Removing your old Window(s).

I. The old window consists of stationary window O, the sliding window X and the division bar. (The division bar holds O in place and needs to be removed).

II. Open the window X all the way and lift the window up and out.

III. Remove the top and bottom screws from the division bar.

IV. Then bang out the division bar with a hammer and a pry-bar or spatula (putty knife).

V. Remove window O by prying the bottom, the top, and the side to loosen it, then lift up and out.

NOTES

Step 6: Installing your Retro Fit Z-Bar (Flush Fin) Window(s).

I. When installing your window(s) you must follow the manufactures installation instructions for warranty purposes.

II. Unpack your window and make sure you always set your window down straight and never on a corner. This is to avoid any damage to the Z-Bar (Flush Fin).

Key Note:

It is good practice to use a level. Place the level on the window frame but not on the track. Make sure to shim the ends of the level first if you need to, then in between for proper support so the frame does not sag when you slide the window open or closed. Then check the sides to make sure they are leveled. If you do this the adjustments you will have to do will be a lot less if any.

NOTES

III. Place your window in the opening and push firmly while someone else screws the window into place. (Be sure to avoid pushing too much because there is a possibility that your Z-Bar (Flush Fin) will bend.

Example:

The arrows indicate the placement for 3" gold screws in the center of the frame.

There should be a 3" space between the top and bottom of the window where the screws are placed. This is only a recommendation.

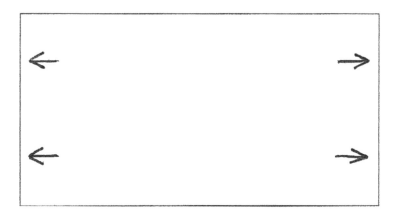

NOTES

IV. Always try to leave the same amount of space on both sides of the window from top to bottom. (This space makes it easier to install your flat trim).

Key Note:

If your home is close to the ocean, it is recommended to use galvanized screws.

You can later paint your screw heads to match the color of your window.

NOTES

V. After you have installed your window(s) you need to check the reveal. (The reveal is the gap that appears when your window is nearly shut). Leaving a ¼" reveal to check for alignment is recommended.

Example:

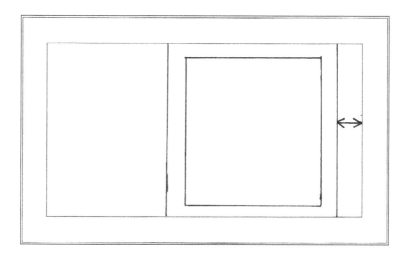

NOTES

VI. If the reveal is even from top to bottom, you are done installing your window. If your reveal is not even, here are some scenarios and solutions.

Example:

A.   B.

A. If the reveal is wider on the bottom than the top, you need to shim on the corner right under the reveal until it is even.
B. If the reveal is wider on the top than the bottom, you need to shim under the division bar until it is even.

Key Note:

The rollers on some windows can be adjusted so you don't have to shim as much.

NOTES

Step 7: Foaming your Retro Fit Window(s).

I. Applying the foam—When applying the foam insulation your goal is to fill in the space between the old and the new window frame. Not the whole cavity.

II. Allow the foam to sit for approximately 15 minutes. Be sure not to wait too long because any over flowing foam will harden and will not be able to be pushed back into the cavity. You can also cut away any excess foam with a utility knife.

NOTES

Step 8: Installing the vinyl trim.

I. Install the top and bottom pieces of trim first. (A & B)

II. Install the side pieces of trim second. (C & D)

Example:

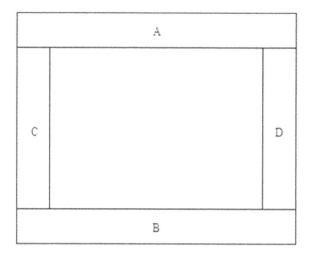

Key Note:

You can use heavy duty snips to cut your trim. (straight cutting snips)

NOTES

Step 9: Sealing your window(s). (inside)

I. If your window trim is white you can use white silicone for windows and doors.

II. If your window trim is another color other than white you can order your trim with its recommended sealant. (silicone, glazing, etc.)

III. Make sure your sealant can also be used outside if not you will have to order another sealant to seal the outside of your window(s).

NOTES

IV. Apply the sealant on the edge of the trim that meets the wall all the way around and were they meet each other.

Example:

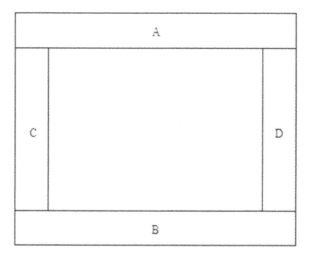

NOTES

IV. If you plan to paint after you are done installing your window(s) make sure that the sealant you are using can be painted before you use it.

Key Note:

You can use your finger to smooth out the sealant and wipe off any excess onto a paper towel. Try not to apply too much pressure and give it a few passes so you don't spread the sealant and make a mess.

NOTES

Step 10: Sealing your window(s). (outside)

I. If your window is white you can use white silicone for windows and doors.

II. If your window is another color other than white you can order your sealant with your trim. (silicone, glazing, etc.)

III. Clear sealant is recommended when applying sealant to the outside of your Window if the exterior color of your home does not match your window.

IV. If you plan to paint after you are done installing your window(s) make sure that the sealant you are using can be painted before you use it.

NOTES

V. Apply the sealant on the sides and top of the window(s), not the bottom so if water gets into the old frame water can still get out and prevents water damage.

VI. For windows that are exposed to heavy rain or do not have an overhang (Roof sticking out over the window), Quad Construction Adhesive is recommended.

You have now successfully installed your Retro Fit Z-Bar (Flush Fin) Window(s).

www.ingramcontent.com/pod-product-compliance
Lightning Source LLC
Chambersburg PA
CBHW051216050326
40689CB00008B/1329